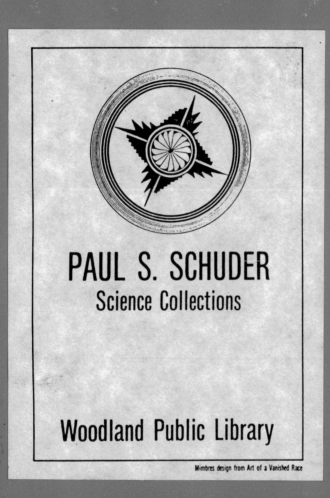

PROFESSOR PROTEIN'S

FITNESS, HEALTH, HYGIENE, AND RELAXATION TONIC

Steve Parker

Illustrated by Rob Shone

COPPER BEECH BOOKS
BROOKFIELD, CONNECTICUT

© Aladdin Books 1996
Produced by
NW Books for
Aladdin Books Ltd
28 Percy Street
London W1P 0LD
First published in the United States in 1996 by
COPPER BEECH BOOKS,
an imprint of The Millbrook Press
2 Old New Milford Road
Brookfield, Connecticut 06804

Concept by David West and Rob Shone
Design David West • Children's Book Design
Editor Jon Richards

STEVE PARKER, the author, is an easy-going, clean-living guy, who proudly possesses a prescription pair of sunglassses. He has written more than 100 books on nature and science for the family.

ROB SHONE, the illustrator, has illustrated a number of children's books and likes nothing better than running a marathon before breakfast.

Cataloging-in-Publication Data is available at the Library of Congress

ISBN 0-7613-0494-0

N⁰2 PROFESSOR

hints and tips on: *exer*CISE

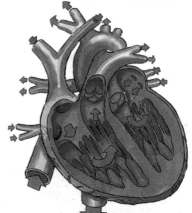

PROTEIN'S CONTENTS

Are you dirty and smelly, and covered in stains and sores? Were your clothes last washed in 1991? Do you eat maggoty meat, drink dishwater, and break wind all the time? Do you prefer spots to sports, and flabby thighs to exercise? Are your muscles weak and floppy, and your teeth full of black holes? Do you get tired just reading all these questions?

Yes?? Then THIS is the BOOK for YOU!

Professor Protein has the low-down on Fitness, Health, Hygiene, And Relaxation. Take his Tonic every day by following the guidelines in this book – and you can't go wrong. Get FHHARTing at once.

PROFESSOR'S FACTS
The science behind the scenes – how and why your body parts and health processes work.

HINTS AND TIPS
Excellent bits of advice that could help you to get the success and riches that you deserve.

BIG TIPS
Even more excellent bits of advice that could help you to find happiness as well as success and riches.

*exer*CISE

Ignore your bicycle, and it gets rusty. Wheels and pedals tighten up, and tires deflate. Ignore your body, and it doesn't get rusty – but joints stiffen, while muscles and bones weaken. So look after yourself. Get fit, stay active – and have fun.

EXERCISE ISN'T JUST FOR JERKS You don't have to be a physical jerk – or do them. Any kind of physical movement or activity counts as exercise, such as funtime at the swimming pool, cycling, dancing, sports like soccer and tennis, racing friends up a hill, skipping along a sun-drenched holiday beach... Anything that gets you moving will also get you fit and healthy, especially if you do it regularly, use lots of muscles, and get slightly out of breath. But, if you laze around like a couch potato, your body will soon start to suffer. Just see the sort of mess you can get into if you don't exercise.

HINTS AND TIPS
SPEED UP SLOWLY

Don't leap straight into a punishing schedule of workouts, sports, and exercises. Begin your activity slowly and carefully. Get advice from someone in the know, like a sports coach. Build up your fitness gradually, over days and weeks. This way, you'll soon improve your physical skills, muscle strength, and coordination. Otherwise, you might end up on the emergency room floor!

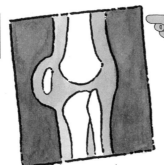

STIFF, PAINFUL JOINTS

Bones are linked by joints. If these aren't moved and flexed regularly, they begin to stiffen. They may bend less, they may hurt more, and they may suffer from bad sprains.

PUFFY, PANTY BREATHING

Breathing, or respiration, is a muscle-powered action. When the breathing muscles in the chest get weak, even ordinary breathing becomes an effort.

FLOPPY, SLOPPY HEARTBEAT

The heart is a bag-shaped lump of powerful muscle. Like any muscle, it benefits from exercise, during which it beats harder and faster. If it doesn't get a workout regularly, then it becomes floppy and sloppy.

WEAK, WEEDY MUSCLES

Muscles that aren't used much become thin, weak, and weedy. They will soon get tired faster and are more likely to become strained, or even tear.

BRITTLE, BAD BONES

Bones need exercise to stay strong and to keep you in one piece (☞ Nº12)! Avoid crutches and plaster casts by staying active.

DON'T OVERDO IT! Many promising world champions, like you, have tried to do too much, too soon. They get carried away with the idea of becoming fit and breaking a world record. They ignore life's other pleasures, like watching a beautiful sunset. This is NOT healthy. One problem is over-use injury, where a body part is forced beyond its natural limits. As you exercise more and become fitter, make sure you stay alert to your body's signals. A pain in the leg? A twinge in the arm? Don't ignore problems – get them solved.

DULL AND BORING

People who are obsessed with something can be boring and tedious. This applies to stamp-collecting, train-watching – and exercise too. Someone who thinks and talks about nothing else can be a real pain!

PROFESSOR'S FACT
MAKE IT AEROBIC

• Aerobic exercise is exercise that uses up lots of oxygen over a long period. To get more oxygen from the air, your lungs have to breathe deeper and quicker. To send more oxygen in the blood to the muscles, your heart has to pump harder and faster. All of this activity is good for both the breathing and heart muscles.

BIG TIP
IT'S GOTTA BE *FUN!*

Make exercise a regular part of your week. Choose something that doesn't need hard-to-get equipment or awkward traveling. Do it with others and make new friends. Above all, have FUN. Then you're more likely to stick with it and get even better.

THE WRONG STUFF

If your activity needs special clothing or equipment, try to get this. You can save money by borrowing or renting, especially from a club. It's better than suffering an accident or injury, due to wearing or using the wrong stuff. You wouldn't go mountaineering in a pair of high heels, would you?

TOO MANY MILES

A car can only go so many miles before it begins to wear out. So can a body – though most of us never get near this "upper limit." The joints are often the first to show signs of wear and tear. This happens sooner if they are twisted into unnatural positions.

GET LEAN AND MEAN WITH A WARM-UP ROUTINE When sports players and athletes jog up and down before the main event, bending and stretching, it's not just for show. It's warm-up time – gentle exercise to loosen muscles, flex joints, and raise heartbeat and breathing rates slightly. Warm-up is not only for superstars, it's for anyone doing exercise. It means that when the real action starts, you are less likely to pull a muscle, sprain a joint, or run out of breath too soon. Warming up is also a good way to detect any small problems, such as a strain, right at the start. Here are a few exercises to get you going.

HEAD AND NECK

Slowly turn head from one side to the other, as far as it will go. Then put your chin on your chest and slowly stretch head up to look at the sky. Repeat these movements several times.

MAIN BODY

Stand up straight, feet slightly apart, arms down by sides. Keeping legs straight, curve backbone to lean left, sliding left hand down left leg. Return to upright, do same on right side. Repeat a few times.

CHEST AND ARMS

Hold arms out sideways, at shoulder height. Swing them forward to touch hands in front, return them to sides. Swing arms up to touch hands above head and then return them to sides. Repeat a number of times.

BACK AND HIPS

Stand up straight, feet together, arms out straight and level. Twist body from hips to neck, to one side, swinging arms around to face behind. Swing back to the front, do same on other side. Repeat several times.

HIPS AND LEGS

Stand upright and step forward with right leg and stretch out left leg behind. Now lean forward on the right leg and hold for a few seconds. Return to standing upright. Continue the exercise, but this time step forward with left leg. Repeat several times.

COOL DOWN, BUT DON'T CHILL OUT After the real action of the main event, take a few minutes to cool down again. Jog slowly. Try stretches and bends that gradually become more gentle. Don't suddenly stop and flop into inaction, or your joints might stiffen and your muscles could tighten. Also, try not to get "too cool." Exercise makes you breathless and hot. The body reacts with cooling processes like sweating and reddened, flushed skin. But these can over-react and the body may get too cold, chilled, and shivery. This can lead to hypothermia, and bad news, as it causes confusion and serious illness.

GENTLE JOG

 Slow running is a good cooling-down exercise. It lets the lungs catch up with obtaining oxygen, and the heart catch up with supplying blood. Yet it still keeps the body slightly active.

SHINY SPACE BLANKET

In extreme conditions, like running a marathon on a cold day, a "space blanket" comes in useful. It's made of thin metal foil that reflects natural body warmth back. Worn like a cloak, it keeps you from getting too cold and allows you to keep moving.

HINTS AND TIPS GEAR CARE

After sports or exercise don't throw all your clothes and equipment into a bag, and forget about them until next time. Keep things aired, washed, and cleaned. Otherwise shoes fester, socks rot, shorts get moldy, and shirts smell. Not something that's good for your image!

PROFESSOR'S FACT OUCH! CRAMP!

• A cramp is a sudden muscle tensing and contraction which you can't control. The muscle becomes hard and tight and it hurts! Cramps are often caused by working muscles too hard when they aren't used to it, or by keeping the body in an awkward posture. To relieve it, gently rub and massage the muscle, while gently stretching the affected body part.

SHAKE IT ALL ABOUT

Cool down by shaking your arms loosely. This relaxes the muscles, frees the joints, and restores normal blood flow to the rest of your body. Bend your neck and back slowly, too. And shake your legs in the same way – one at a time, of course.

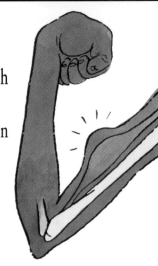

STRENGTH IS THE FIRST OF THE THREE S's Top-class athletes and sports players know about the Three S's for fitness and health. These are Strength, Suppleness, and Stamina. Professor Protein would like us to start with Strength. STRENGTH is mainly down to your muscles. These are parts of the body that can get shorter, or contract. Every body has the same number of main muscles. They are called skeletal muscles, because they pull on and move the bones of the skeleton. Exercise does not give you more muscles. But it does make your existing muscles stronger, and less likely to get injured or tired.

1 WHOLE MUSCLE
A typical muscle is long, with a bulging middle called the belly. Its ends taper into ropelike parts called tendons. These are attached firmly to bones.

2 BUNDLES OF FIBERS
Muscles are split into bundles called fascicles. Each bundle contains about 100 to 200 tiny, stringlike muscle fibers, called myofibers.

3 MUSCLE FIBER
This is a single, long cell, 0.004 inches across. Big muscles have more fibers. A large leg muscle has 1,000 fibers that are up to 12 inches (30 cm) long. A tiny muscle has 20 fibers only a few inches long.

4 MUSCLE FIBRILS
Each muscle fiber is a bundle of even smaller, thinner parts called muscle fibrils (myofibrils). And each fibril is made of even smaller parts, muscle filaments. These are really giant protein molecules, actin and myosin.

5 MUSCLE FILAMENTS
The thick muscle filaments are myosin, the thin ones are actin. These slide past each other, using millions of microscopic pulling movements. As a result, the entire muscle gets shorter, pulling on the bone that it is attached to.

PROFESSOR'S FACTS
MYRIAD MUSCLES
• Each human body has about 640 skeletal muscles (plus other types of muscles found in inner parts like the heart and intestines, as the Professor explains later). Every muscle has a scientific name, which is usually long and difficult to ~~sepl slep~~ spell. The body's largest muscle is the one you sit on, the gluteus maximus in the buttock. The smallest muscle is the stapedius, about as thin as a hair, that sits deep inside your ear.

MUSCLES ARE STRONG, BUT THEY CAN GO WRONG In a thin, weak person, the thin and floppy muscles make up about one-third of the total body weight. In a strong and super-fit person (like you), the rippling, bulging muscles make up almost one-half of the total body weight. The extra size and power comes from thicker fibers inside each muscle. However, muscles must be exercised carefully and strength built up gradually. If you try to do too much, too soon, then your muscles and the surrounding tissues can suffer damage such as a strain, pull, or tear (see below).

PULLED MUSCLE

Too much strain on a muscle pulls it too hard, and tears some of its microscopic fibers. This makes the muscle weak, tender to touch, and painful to use. The remedy is rest, massage, and support from a bandage.

HERNIA

This is a bulge of soft inner parts, like intestines, that pokes through or between muscle layers and makes a lump under the skin. Hernias happen at "weak points" such as around the navel or in the groin. Hernias can also affect people of all ages – not just the old.

PROFESSOR'S FACT
MUSCLE MOUSE

• The word "muscle" comes from the ancient Latin word *musculus*, which means "little mouse." This is because the bulges and ripples of strong muscles look like a mouse running along under the skin. (Honest!)

TORN TENDON

If part of the body is moved violently, the wrench may tear the ropelike fibers that attach the muscle to the bone, called the tendon. If the tendon tears away from its anchorage point on the bone, this is more serious. It may require surgery.

HINTS AND TIPS
MORE SKILL, MORE MUSCLE POWER

Brute strength and muscle power are useful. But so are technique, coordination, balance, and skill. A small person who practices weight-lifting can lift heavier weights than a big person who doesn't practice.

TOUGH ON THE INSIDE A skyscraper is held up by a steel skeleton – a supporting frame of girders and plates. So is the body, except its skeleton is made from bone (which is almost as strong as steel but 10 times lighter). Most of the joints between the bones are flexible, unlike the rigid, welded joints in a skyscraper. Bones also need plenty of minerals and nutrients from healthy food, whereas a skyscraper can't even eat.

HINTS AND TIPS
HEALTHY BONES

Bones are not dull and dry. They are very alive, with their own blood vessels, nerves, and other supplies. Exercise helps to make them strong and healthy, while a good diet keeps them that way (☞ Nº41).

PROFESSOR'S FACTS
NO BONE ALONE

• There are 206 bones in a human skeleton. The biggest are the thigh bones, or femurs. The smallest are the stirrup bones inside each ear. More than half the body's bones (106) are in the feet, wrists, hands, and ankles.

BIG TIP
KEEP MOVING

Your bones are always changing their structure to cope with everyday strains and pressure. Without this change the bone becomes brittle and is liable to snap after an innocent jolt. So keep those bones moving!

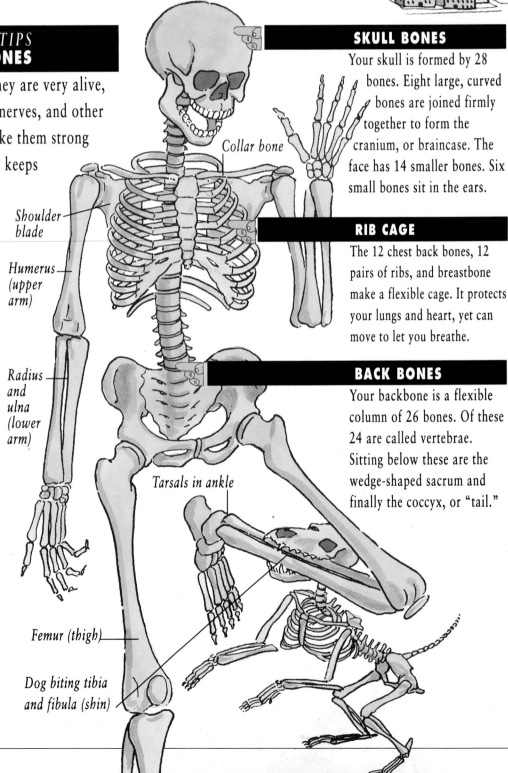

Collar bone

Shoulder blade

Humerus (upper arm)

Radius and ulna (lower arm)

Tarsals in ankle

Femur (thigh)

Dog biting tibia and fibula (shin)

SKULL BONES

Your skull is formed by 28 bones. Eight large, curved bones are joined firmly together to form the cranium, or braincase. The face has 14 smaller bones. Six small bones sit in the ears.

RIB CAGE

The 12 chest back bones, 12 pairs of ribs, and breastbone make a flexible cage. It protects your lungs and heart, yet can move to let you breathe.

BACK BONES

Your backbone is a flexible column of 26 bones. Of these 24 are called vertebrae. Sitting below these are the wedge-shaped sacrum and finally the coccyx, or "tail."

THE SECOND OF THE THREE S's IS SUPPLENESS This involves the movable joints between bones. Each joint has its own mechanical design, such as a hinge or a ball-and-socket. Healthy, supple joints bend and flex easily over their natural range of movements without stiffness or pain. GOOD exercise keeps joints "flexupple." But BAD exercise bends joints in twisted, unnatural ways. This can cause sprains and even dislocations. Some tips below will tell you how to exercise these joints and keep them supple into old age.

BIG TIP
SPRAIN PAIN

A sprain happens when a joint is pushed, pulled, or twisted, beyond its natural movement. The ligaments and joint capsule become stretched, swollen, and sore and may even tear. The main remedy is rest and a bandage (not too tight). Many sprains happen when the joint has been wrenched violently or by somebody hitting you very hard.

So don't be vain, use your brain, and train to avoid pain from a sprain.

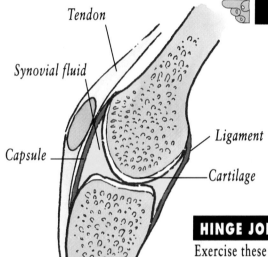

Tendon

Synovial fluid

Capsule

Ligament

Cartilage

INSIDE A JOINT

While they might appear tough, your joints contain many delicate parts that can be damaged by over-exertion. Cartilage, a substance that coats the ends of the bones and helps them move smoothly, can be torn by sudden twists. Avoid over-exerting joints to keep them moving smoothly.

HINGE JOINT

Exercise these joints by flexing limbs, such as your elbows and knees, to keep them supple. A hinge joint will only move back and forth in one direction.

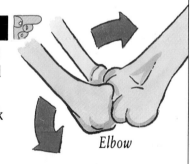

Elbow

GLIDING JOINTS

Two fairly flat surfaces slide and glide over one another, as in the foot and wrist. Although they don't move much, these joints should still be exercised to keep them flexible.

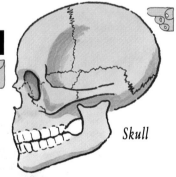

Skull

SUTURE JOINTS

Some joints cannot move at all. Skull bones are fused together, attached firmly along suture joints. Sadly, you can't really exercise them.

Foot

BALL-AND-SOCKET JOINT

Swinging your legs and arms will exercise these joints in the hips and shoulders. Make sure you exercise them through their entire range of movement.

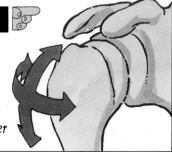

Shoulder

A BREATH OF FRESH AIR In fact, fresh air is essential for exercise, and for all other body actions, from chopping wood to cutting toenails. Why? Your body needs energy for living. It gets this energy from food (☞ №38), but it needs oxygen, a gas found in air, to release this energy. Oxygen makes up one-fifth of the air around us. You breathe air into your lungs, where oxygen is absorbed into your blood, and you stay alive.

Nasal cavity

NOSE

The nose sniffs, snuffles, and smells. Slimy mucus (the polite word for *snot*) in the nasal cavity, traps dust and other stuff. Get rid of these by blowing your nose regularly.

THROAT

The throat is a passage for air into the windpipe as you breathe, and for food into the gullet as you eat. Don't eat as you exercise, or the two may get mixed up and cause you to choke!

WINDPIPE

This tube leads from your throat down to your lungs. The voice-box, or larynx, is just below it, and lets you shout as loud as you want.

AIRWAYS

The windpipe splits into two airways, called bronchi, one for each lung. These will divide, like a tree's branches, into smaller air tubes.

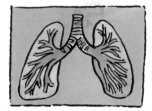

Windpipe

HINTS AND TIPS
WARM, CLEAN, DAMP

Air breathed in through the nose gets warmed, filtered, and moistened. This is better for the lungs, compared to air breathed in through the mouth. However, during exercise you need to get extra oxygen into your body, so you breathe through both your nose and mouth.

OUT WITH THE BAD AIR, IN WITH THE GOOD Deep inside the lungs are millions of tiny air bubbles, called alveoli. In these bubbles, oxygen passes from the air, into the blood, and is carried around the body for use in energy production. As part of this energy production, the body makes a waste product, called carbon dioxide. If it's not removed, it could be harmful. It's collected by the blood, and passes into the air in the lungs. Once here, it can be safely removed from your body simply by breathing out.

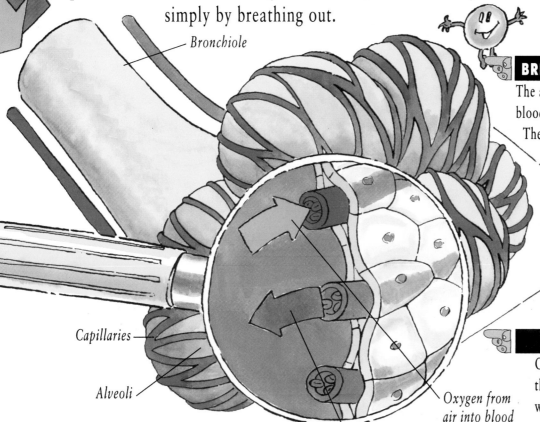

Bronchiole

Capillaries

Alveoli

Oxygen from air into blood

Carbon dioxide from blood into air

BRINGING BLOOD

The alveoli are surrounded by blood vessels, called capillaries. These carry a stream of blood into and out of the lungs.

FAIR EXCHANGE

Oxygen seeps from the air in the alveoli, through their thin walls, into the blood in the capillaries. At the same time, carbon dioxide goes the other way to get breathed out.

PROFESSOR'S FACTS
ANYONE FOR TENNIS?

• How do you fit a tennis court into your chest? Although they are small, there are 700 million alveoli packed into your lungs, giving the body a huge area through which it can absorb oxygen. In fact, if all your alveoli were spread out flat, they would cover a tennis court.

BIG TIP
CIGS ARE DRAGS

Breathing airways and lungs hate tobacco smoke. It clogs them with thick tar, causes breathlessness, smoker's cough, increases the risks of chest infection, and can harm the heart and blood vessels. It also makes cancer more likely in the lungs, mouth, and other places.

BREATHING IS POWERED BY MUSCLES

Like all body movements, breathing in happens when muscles get shorter, or contract (☞ Nº10). The muscles involved are the diaphragm under the lungs and those between the ribs, called the intercostal muscles. The important thing about breathing is you have to keep doing it to get rid of stale air, and breathe in fresh supplies. This means your breathing muscles have to work 24 hours a day.

BIG TIP
BIG BREATHS

If you get very short of breath, bend forward slightly, hands on hips. This position makes breathing easier. It uses the muscles in your neck, shoulders, and abdomen to help the normal breathing muscles.

PROFESSOR'S FACTS
HOW MUCH AIR? - 1

• At rest, the volume of air you breathe in and out is 1 pint (half a liter). With an average breathing rate of 12 to 15 breaths each minute, you will breathe about 12 pints (6 liters) of air every 60 seconds.

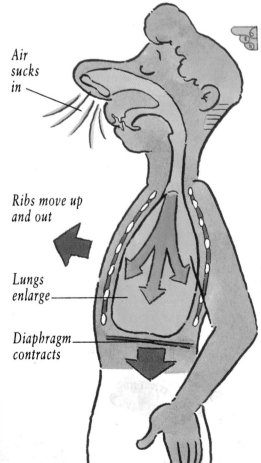

Air sucks in

Ribs move up and out

Lungs enlarge

Diaphragm contracts

BREATHING IN

Like a set of bellows, your lungs are pulled apart by the diaphragm and your rib cage, sucking in the air you need. For normal breathing, this movement is not very big. But when a lot of air is needed, then your ribs will move up and out a lot to draw in the extra air.

BREATHING OUT

This is a simple affair – you just relax. The rib cage falls back to its resting position and your diaphragm relaxes. Together, these movements squeeze your lungs, decreasing their volume and pushing the "stale" air out of them.

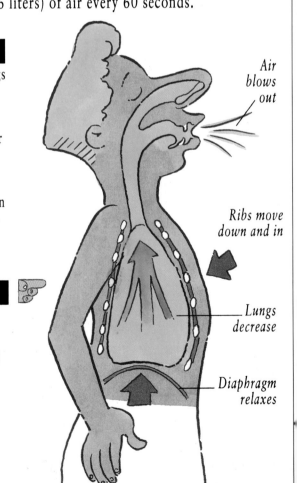

Air blows out

Ribs move down and in

Lungs decrease

Diaphragm relaxes

FASTER AND DEEPER As soon as you start to exercise, your muscles begin to use up more oxygen. You need to breathe faster and deeper, to get extra air into your lungs. This puts extra oxygen into your blood, which flows away to spread the oxygen all around the body (☞ Nº18). Active muscles also make more carbon dioxide, but luckily the faster, deeper breathing gets rid of it. So get moving, and work those breathing muscles to improve the third of the "S's" – STAMINA.

PROFESSOR'S FACTS
HOW MUCH AIR? - 2

After exercise, your breathing volume can rise to more than 8 pints (4 l) and the breathing rate to 60 breaths per minute. This means you breathe 480 pints (240 l) of air each minute. That's 40 times the amount at rest!

HINTS AND TIPS
FORCE IT OUT

Help your lungs get rid of stale air by forced expiration. As you breathe out, make your tummy or abdominal muscles tense and tight. These will press on your lungs from below, forcing more air out.

BREATHING STAMINA

Exercise makes muscles fitter and stronger. This includes breathing muscles. As they get more powerful, they make breathing more effective. You take in more oxygen over longer periods. This increases your stamina.

BREATHING RHYTHM

As you exercise, try to breathe in time with your body movements or actions. This helps the rhythm of both moving and breathing.

BREATHING PROBLEMS

Some people are prone to asthma or similar breathing problems. They should always have a suitable inhaler, or similar medication handy, just in case.

AND NOW, THE HEART OF THE MATTER Breathing gets vital oxygen into the lungs, so you can stay alive. But how does oxygen get to the rest of your body? This is where blood comes in – and goes out. It flows from the lungs to the heart. This powerful pump forces it out all around the body, from head to toe. As the heart pumps, approximately once each second or faster, it makes a "lub-dup" sound. How does it make this sound? See below.

BIG TIP HEALTHY HEART

The heart's walls are almost solid muscle. It's a special type of muscle called cardiac muscle or myocardium, and it never gets tired. Like other muscles, it gets stronger and fitter with exercise. This is yet another huge reason why you need to exercise.

THE TWO-PART HEART

A heart is two pumps joined together. The left pump sends blood all around the body, delivering oxygen and picking up carbon dioxide. This blood returns to the right pump, which sends it to the lungs for more oxygen, then back to the left pump, and so on, and so on ...

PUMPING CHAMBERS

Blood enters the heart from thin-walled vessels called veins. These flow into the upper chambers on either side, called the atria. From here the blood is pushed into the lower chambers, called the ventricles. These force the blood under great pressure up into thick-walled vessels called arteries.

PROFESSOR'S FACTS WHY "LUB-DUP"?

• This is the sound of a heart beating. Hear it by putting your ear on a friend's chest. A doctor may use a stethoscope. The noises are the one-way valves slapping closed. This stops blood from flowing the wrong way.

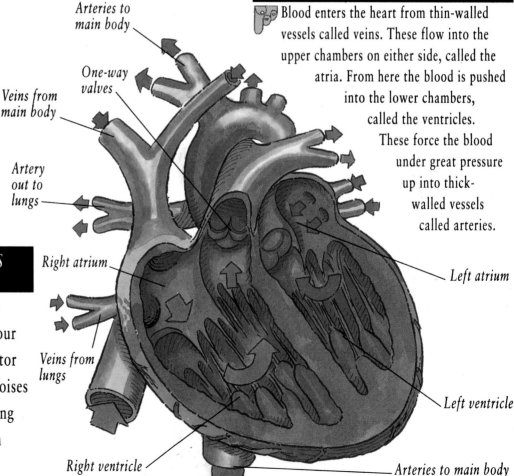

Arteries to main body

One-way valves

Veins from main body

Artery out to lungs

Right atrium

Left atrium

Veins from lungs

Left ventricle

Right ventricle

Arteries to main body

KEEP YOUR FINGER ON THE PULSE Every beat of your heart forces blood under great pressure out into the main arteries. The surge makes bulges pass along the artery walls. You can feel these bulges, or pulses, at various places around your body, especially where arteries cross over bones and joints. Most convenient is the radial artery in the wrist. Checking your pulse rate is a good way to monitor your fitness level (see below).

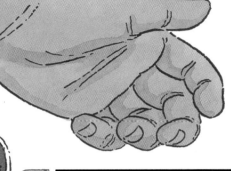

1 FIND YOUR PULSE

Put your finger on the side of your wrist, below the thumb mound. Feel between the hard, cordlike tendons for the pulsing artery.

2 COUNT YOUR PULSE RATE

The pulse rate is the number of beats per minute. So you'll need a watch. Count the pulses in half a minute, then double this number (to save time). This is your resting pulse rate.

3 EXERCISE

Do five minutes of strenuous exercise, such as fast jogging, then stop. Take your pulse rate every minute until it's returned to your resting rate. The time it takes to do this is your recovery time.

4 GET FIT!

Now do lots of exercise and get fit. Repeat steps 1, 2, and 3. Is your recovery time shorter? This shows how well your heart copes with the extra work, and is a guide to general fitness. The shorter the time, the fitter you are.

PROFESSOR'S FACTS WHY BEAT FASTER?

• When you exercise, your muscles are busier. They need more oxygen and other supplies which the blood brings. So the heart beats faster, to send more blood to the muscles.

HINTS AND TIPS PULSE RATES

These are average resting pulse rates, per minute:

• *7 years 80-85* • *10 years 75-80* • *Adult 65-75*
But remember, no one is truly average, so this is just a general guide for you to use.

DON'T OVERDO IT! Run, push, puff, rush, pant, whoa! Too much! Slow down. Breathless? Muscles tired? Joints aching? No wonder, if you try to run a marathon with no practice. Your body will soon tell you when it's had enough. Like any complicated, well-tuned machine, the human being has its limits. If you try to push beyond them, the red warning light comes on: *STOP!* Take notice. Exercise gradually and practice more, to improve your fitness. It'll take days and weeks – but it's the best way to do it!

OUT OF BREATH

When you're active, you breathe faster, to get extra oxygen for the working muscles. But there's a limit. So work up to it, and try to raise it slowly. Don't exercise and pant so hard that you get dizzy or sick.

CRAMP

This is when a muscle contracts by itself. It becomes hard and stiff – and hurts! It's due to the buildup of a waste chemical, lactic acid, in the muscle. (☞ №9 and see how to relieve the pain.)

BIG TIP SHOE OFF!

Get shooed! Wear comfortable sneakers or running shoes, with the right padding and sole support. You won't run far in high-heeled pumps!

SORE FEET

If your shoes don't fit, or they wear out, then you may get sore feet, raw spots, and painful blisters. Sweaty socks cause sores, too (☞ №34).

STITCH IN TIME

This is a sharp pain under the ribs. Doctors aren't sure why this happens, but it may be due to your diaphragm not receiving enough oxygen and tiring very quickly, causing the sharp pain in your side.

PROFESSOR'S FACT GET IN A SWEAT

• Your body must get rid of the extra heat it makes as you exercise. The microscopic sweat glands in your skin ooze watery sweat through their pores onto the surface. It dries and evaporates, drawing heat from the body.

Evaporating sweat reduces the hot body's temperature.

Sweat pore

Sweat gland

personal HYGIENE

Your body is a giant zoo – home to millions of living things. Most are terribly tiny, and happily harmless. But some aren't.

Find out how to blast the nasties with their deadly enemies, Soap'n'Water!

UNDER YOUR SKIN Like the rest of the body, skin is made of microscopic cells. On the skin's surface the cells are flat, hard, and tough for protection, like tiles stuck on a roof. As you move around, sit, walk, wash, get dry, and sleep in your bed, these cells are worn away and rubbed off your body. On average, you lose about 50,000 every second. Scratch your cheek – there go another few million! But don't panic, your skin won't disappear. Just under the surface, more cells are multiplying like mad, to replace the ones that have been rubbed off.

AT THE SURFACE

The outer layer of skin is called the epidermis. The hard, flattened cells on its surface are not very lively. In fact they are dead, ready to be rubbed away.

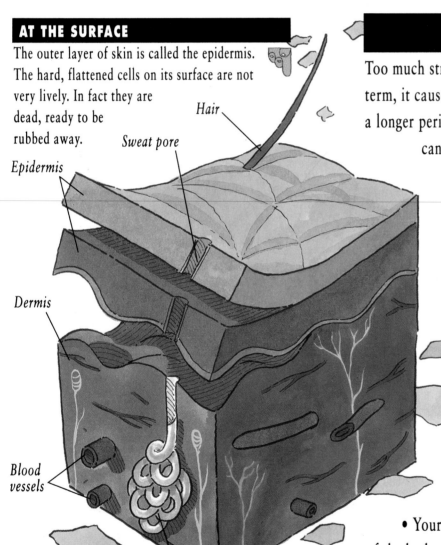

Hair

Sweat pore

Epidermis

Dermis

Blood vessels

Sweat gland

BIG TIP
CARE IN THE SUN

Too much strong sunlight damages skin. In the short term, it causes the soreness and pain of sunburn. Over a longer period it may trigger skin growths and cancers. So Slip-Slap-Slop. Slip on a shirt or top, slap on a wide sunhat, and slop on the sunscreen lotion.

JUST UNDER THE SURFACE

At the base of the epidermis, cells are busy multiplying. They move upward, and get filled with keratin which makes them very hard. After three weeks they reach the surface to replace those that have been rubbed off.

PROFESSOR'S FACT
SKIN IS THIN

• Your skin's thickness varies on different parts of the body. On the soles of the feet it's more than 1/20th inch (five millimeters) thick. On the eyelids it's less than 1/100th inch (half a millimeter) thick and very delicate. So don't try walking on your eyelids!

EVEN DEEPER UNDER THE SURFACE

The lower layer of skin is the dermis. It contains millions of microscopic touch receptors, nerves, blood vessels, hairs, and sweat pores.

HAVE YOU HAD A BATH TODAY? No? Eeek! Human skin is not self-cleaning, like an oven. It needs to be washed, all over. To do this, use soap and warm water, as found in most bathrooms. Splash the warm water onto your skin, rub on the soap to make a bubbly lather, scrub well, and wash off the sweat, dirt, and grime. If you've never seen soap before, it usually comes in small bars or lumps, often green or pink, sometimes with writing. Or use gel or a similar soapy substitute. If you don't use them, your skin will get dirty, grimy, sore, spotty, and smelly.

PROFESSOR'S FACT
HOW SOAP WORKS

• Tiny pieces of dirt clump together in larger sticky lumps, which you can see. Soap is a type of chemical substance called a detergent. It surrounds each tiny piece of dirt, making it come away from the main lump and away from your skin. Gradually the dirt clump is broken into millions of specks that float away when they are rinsed off.

TOP TO BOTTOM

Wash all over, not just the parts that show! Especially under arms, between legs, and in folds of skin. Sweat and dirt are more likely to collect here, trapping dirt and causing smells.

USING A SPONGE

Dunk the sponge in the water, and squeeze it to get the air out and water in. Then rub it on the soap, and rub it on you.

DON'T GET OLD SWEAT

Skin makes sweat, a watery, salty fluid with an important job – to keep the body cool in hot conditions. It also makes sebum, the natural waxy oil which makes skin supple and water-repellent. But as sweat and sebum dry, they become smelly and attract dirt. A good reason to bathe regularly.

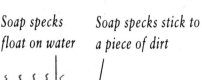

Soap specks float on water

Soap specks stick to a piece of dirt

Soap specks surround a piece of dirt

SKIN GETS SPOTTY But what kinds of spots are they, and what do they mean? Some types of spots and pimples are caused by poor hygiene – not washing properly or often enough. Other kinds of spots are due to a general body-wide infection by germs, like measles or chickenpox. There's not a lot you can do about these, as they are part of the illness. Some people get spots as they grow and develop fast during puberty, when they enter their teens. Also some spots are... ☞

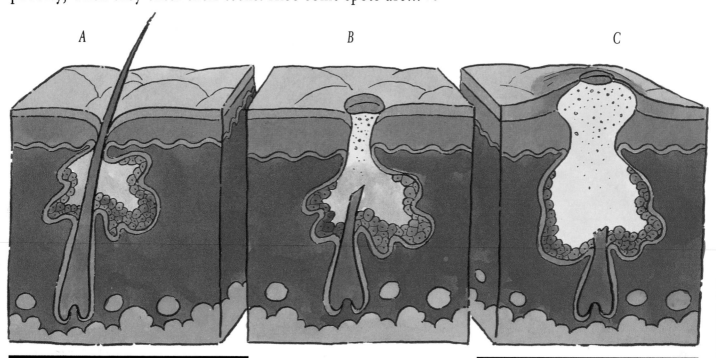

A B C

SPOT NO.1 - THE BLACKHEAD

Some spots form in pits in the skin from which hairs grow, called hair follicles (A). The follicle gets blocked by a plug of natural skin oil or grease (B). This collects dirt and looks dark. The natural oils build up underneath, making the spot raised (C).

A RASH DECISION

Measles, chickenpox, rubella, and similar infectious diseases produce various types of skin rash. In addition to the rash, you usually feel ill with other symptoms of the illness, such as a fever or coughing.

SPOT NO.2 - THE BOIL

A boil develops in much the same way as a blackhead, when dirt, oil, or wax blocks one of the hair follicles. However, there are also germs involved – usually the bacteria called *Staphylococcus*. They infect the spot, making it red, swollen with pus, and very tender.

SPOT NO.3 - THE WART

A wart is a small patch of skin infected by a virus. The skin develops a tiny cauliflower-like lump with small black specks inside, which are clotted blood vessels. Wart paint or cream from the pharmacist will soon get rid of it.

☞ ... Bites or stings, made by tiny, pesty creatures such as mosquitoes, fleas, lice, ticks, wasps, and so on. Or they may be due to touching plants such as nettles or primrose. Some people have very sensitive skin and break out in spots when they touch certain things, like detergents. There are also birthmarks, freckles, and moles. Very rarely, a spot or mark may mean something more serious, like a skin growth. If in doubt, visit the expert spot-spotter – your local doctor. Unsightly marks can be hidden with makeup, frozen, snipped, or injected (☞ Nº34 for more spots).

PROFESSOR'S FACT
SKIN ALLERGIES

• Some people are extra-sensitive to substances in soaps, paints, varnishes, plants, foods, and even certain metals like nickel (but not schoolwork). When these are touched, the skin becomes red and blotchy, perhaps itchy, and blistered. This is called contact eczema or contact dermatitis. Hypo-allergenic skin cream helps to soothe this problem.

SPOT NO.4 – THE FRECKLE

This is simply a small area of skin with slightly more of the skin-coloring substance, melanin, than the skin around it. Melanin is the stuff that makes you suntanned. Freckles are usually most noticeable on the face, hands, and arms. They become darker in sunshine, like small patches of suntan.

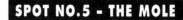

SPOT NO.5 – THE MOLE

A mole is like a freckle, but more so. It's a small area of skin that contains even more melanin than the skin around it. Moles are generally harmless. However, if they change in some way (see below), check with the doctor.

BIG TIP
EARLIER = BETTER

See the doctor if you're worried about a skin spot or mark, especially if:
• it itches
• it bleeds
• it grows
• it persists.
Probably, there's nothing to worry about. But if it's a growth of some kind, early treatment is best.

SPOT NO.6 – THE BIRTHMARK

A bookmark shows the page you are reading, when you close the book. A birthmark is different. It's usually a dense collection of tiny blood vessels in the skin, called a nevus. An unsightly birthmark can be removed by special treatment with a laser, or merely covered up with makeup.

HAIR TODAY, GONE TOMORROW The average person has about 125,000 hairs on his or her head. Every day, around 60 fall out. Don't panic, this does not mean that you're going bald. In most younger people, the hairs that fall out are replaced by new ones. There are hairs all over your body, but they only grow thick enough to be easily noticed on the scalp (and a few other places). Hair is made from the protein called keratin, which also makes up your nails and outer layer of skin. It also forms the hooves, claws, and horns of many animals!

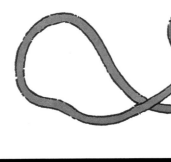

PROFESSOR'S FACT
HAIR COLOR

• Hairs get their color from melanin, the same coloring substance that gives your skin its tan. You can tint or dye the hair shafts lots of different shades. But as the hairs continue to grow from their roots, they'll always go back to their natural color.

HAIR SHAFT

This is like a rod made of flattened cells squashed together. A strand of hair is just as strong as an equally thick strand of copper.

HAIR FOLLICLE

The shape of the follicle opening determines whether the hair is straight, wavy, or curly. A round opening produces straight hair, an oval opening produces wavy hair, and a spiral-shaped opening produces curly hair.

DANDRUFF

This is not a hair problem. It's the over-production of tiny skin flakes from the scalp. To treat it use a medicated shampoo, and be sure to follow the instructions carefully.

BIG TIP
CLEVER COMBING

Start brushing or combing toward the ends of the hairs, to get rid of tangles along the shafts. Gradually comb closer to the roots. If you start at the roots, you comb tangles together along the hairs, into tight and troublesome knots.

HAIR ROOT

The root, sitting inside the follicle, is the only living part of the hair. Cells multiply continuously to make the base of the shaft longer, gradually pushing it up and out. Once this growing stops, the hair will die and fall out.

WE SPEND MILLIONS ON HAIR CARE Which might seem odd – so much money on something that's dead! You can change your appearance a lot by changing your hairstyle – the way the hairs are cut, combed, and perhaps colored and held by gel or mousse. But any head of hair benefits from basic hygiene, including a wash, brush, and trim. Likewise, nails need cleaning and trimming. Or they can get dirty, broken, infected, and painful.

WASHING
We wash hair to get rid of dirt, dust, tangles, old skin waxes and oils, dried sweat, old gels, creams, mousses, and other hair treatments, and maybe pests, like lice or fleas. There are hundreds of shampoos to choose from. In general, once every day or so is enough.

HOW A NAIL GROWS
Nails, like hairs and skin, are almost completely dead and formed from cells filled with keratin. The only growing part is the root, just under the surface, in a small fold of skin.

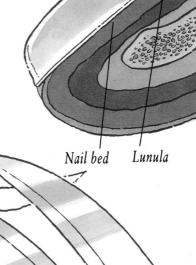

Cuticle

Nail root

Finger bone

Nail bed Lunula

The "moon" part or lunula is where the nail is stuck firmly to the skin beneath.

TRIMMING NAILS
Untrimmed nails crack, fray, and break. Trim them with nail-scissors or nail-clippers, following the nail's curve. Do this after a shower or bath, when they are clean and slightly softer. Don't cut into the skin or it will hurt, and it may bleed and get infected.

HINTS AND TIPS
SPLIT ENDS
Washing, brushing, and general wear make hair ends frayed and ragged – "split ends." This can look untidy. A quick trim snips off the split ends, without slowing the hair growth. Hairs grow about 0.4 inches (one mm) every three days.

GREASY HAIR
Some people have hair that looks flat and greasy. It's not a disease, it just happens to be natural for them. A shampoo especially for greasy hair is the easy answer.

BIG TIP
NAIL-NIBBLING
The short answer is — don't bite your nails! This includes fingernails and toenails. It makes them more likely to break or get infected, and it doesn't look good.

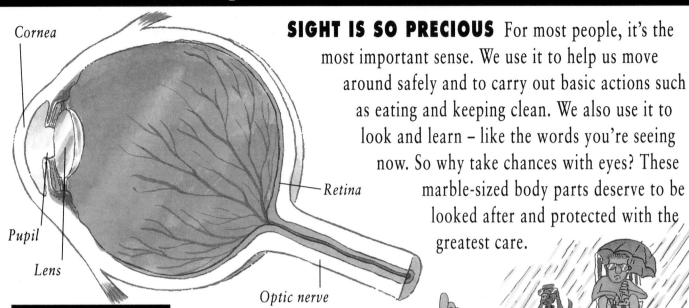

Cornea

Pupil

Lens

Retina

Optic nerve

SIGHT IS SO PRECIOUS For most people, it's the most important sense. We use it to help us move around safely and to carry out basic actions such as eating and keeping clean. We also use it to look and learn – like the words you're seeing now. So why take chances with eyes? These marble-sized body parts deserve to be looked after and protected with the greatest care.

PROFESSOR'S FACT
EYE STRAIN

• Eyes may get tired, sore, and achy due to:

• Too much bright light, causing you to squint a lot. Get some shade!

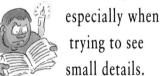

• Too much dim light, especially when trying to see small details. Turn more light on!

• A visual condition such as far-sightedness. See an optician!

• A medical condition such as an eye infection. See a doctor!

EYE PROTECTORS

A visor, goggles, or some other eye protection is sensible for anything that involves flying pieces or splashed drips. It could be sanding wood, processing food, grinding metal, or mixing paint.

EXTRA EYE LENSES

Glasses or contact lenses help the eye's own lens to focus properly, so you can see clearly. Blurred, misty, or unclear vision can lead to accidents and injury. In some situations, like driving a vehicle, it's against the law!

EYES COOL IN THE SUNSHINE

Sunglasses look cool, and they help eyes too. The right kinds of sunglasses cut down glare and stop harmful ultraviolet light from reaching the eyes.

BIG TIP
EYES RIGHT?

Have an eye examination every year, even if things seem fine. The optician, or ophthalmologist, can detect early signs of trouble and give better treatment. Also, you may not notice a change in your eyesight, until you try to read the smaller and smaller letters on the test chart.

THE BODY HAS SEVERAL SETS OF HOLES Ear-holes let in sound waves, so we can hear. Nose holes let in air, so we can breathe. Holes naturally collect lint, dust, dirt, and germs, and the occasional small pests, like a midge or gnat. However, these holes have their own natural cleaning mechanisms. So we don't have to do much except keep an eye on them – using a mirror, of course.

GO NO FURTHER THAN THE DOTTED LINE

Ear canal

Q-tip

External ear

Ear hole

PROTECTING EARS

Ear defenders help to keep out dust, dirt, and loud noise. Too much loud noise, especially from headphones, can harm the delicate inner ear and cause deafness. So LISTEN to the warnings – while you still can.

EARACHE

There are many possible causes of earache, from a cold, to accumulated ear wax, to severe ear infection. Don't poke things into the ear and don't take chances with your sense of hearing. Consult the doctor for a proper diagnosis.

CLEANING EARS

Wash in, around, and behind the ear flap (pinna) as normal. If the ear hole itself looks grimy, wash around it with a Q-tip. But don't poke anything deeper into the ear canal.

BLEEDIN' NOSE

The nose lining has a very rich blood supply, to warm incoming air. Even a slight knock can start a nosebleed. Lean forward and pinch just below the bridge of the nose for 10 minutes, while breathing through your mouth. Then try not to blow the nose for the next few hours.

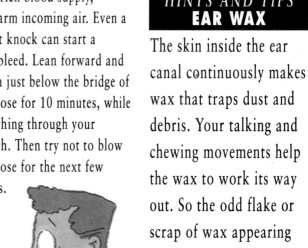

EAR FLOSS

BIG TIP
NOSE-BLOWING

Nasal mucus (snot) is designed to trap germs and dust. Don't sniff it back in – blow it out, preferably into a tissue. And don't blow too hard, as this could damage the nose lining and may cause a nosebleed. The infection that causes your cold may spread to other mucus layers, such as those in your ears and throat.

HINTS AND TIPS
EAR WAX

The skin inside the ear canal continuously makes wax that traps dust and debris. Your talking and chewing movements help the wax to work its way out. So the odd flake or scrap of wax appearing from the ear hole is perfectly OK!

CHOMP, CHEW, CRUSH, MUNCH Our teeth are amazing. Day after day, they chew and mash the meals we eat, even very hard foods like nuts. The gums around them give living support in this hard work. But teeth and gums are also vulnerable. They can be attacked by rotting food and multiplying germs. So oral hygiene – clean and healthy teeth, gums, and mouth – is very important.

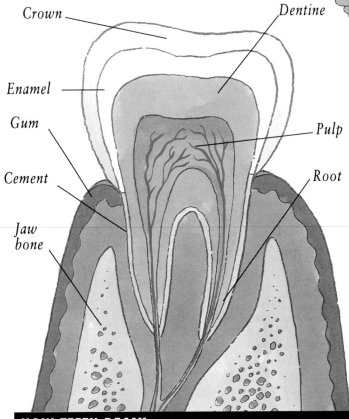

Crown
Dentine
Enamel
Gum
Cement
Pulp
Root
Jaw bone

INSIDE A TOOTH

The hardest, whitest part of the tooth is the enamel. This covers the outside of the top part – the crown. Beneath it is a slightly softer, shock-absorbing layer of dentine. Inside is the pulp of blood vessels and nerves. The tooth root is fixed into the jaw bone by natural cement.

BIG TIP DENTISTS ARE NICE!

Have a dental checkup every 6 or 12 months, or as your dentist advises. The dentist can give you advice on cleaning teeth, and see how they are developing. He or she can also detect and repair any decay before it becomes too serious. So don't be afraid. This won't hurt a bit...

PROFESSOR'S FACT THE MOST COMMON DISEASE

• What's the most common health problem in many countries? Colds? Backaches? No, it's dental decay, or caries, and gum disease, or gingivitis. It's due partly to eating too much sweet, sugary food.

HOW TEETH DECAY

When teeth aren't brushed or cleaned, bits of food get stuck on or between them (1). Bacterial germs feast on the sugars in this old food, making it rotten and forming sticky plaque (2). As the bacteria feed, they make a chemical waste product called acid, which eats into the enamel (3). The acid slowly erodes a hole or cavity in the dentine too (4). As the erosion reaches the pulp it causes painful toothache.

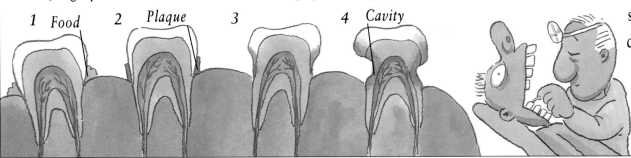

1 Food   2 Plaque   3   4 Cavity

BRUSH, FLOSS, SWISH, WASH Someone who's obsessed with oral hygiene could brush their teeth, floss between them, and swish mouthwash around, about five times a day. For others, brushing two or three times daily after meals – ALWAYS before bedtime – is the best they can do. But it's time well spent. And use the right equipment – cleaning your teeth with a spoon might be dangerous! Otherwise it could mean years of tooth decay, having teeth drilled and filled, having them taken out...

BIG TIP
DON'T HIDE THE FLUORIDE

Fluoride is a natural chemical that helps to strengthen teeth against decay. It's already in many water supplies, or it's added at the water treatment facilities. Check with your dentist, who should recommend that you use a fluoride toothpaste as well.

1 BRUSHING

Use plenty of toothpaste. Brush from side to side, and up and down, and around and around, so that you rub every surface of every tooth in every direction – especially between the teeth and where they meet the gums.

HINTS AND TIPS
SEE HOW CLEAN

Disclosing tablets show how good you are at cleaning your teeth. They dye or color bits of plaque. Follow the instructions and see if you are not properly cleaning any of your teeth and gums when you brush.

2 FLOSSING

Floss is thin stringy stuff that slides between the teeth. You pull it back and forth with a sawing action to remove pieces of lodged food and other debris that may be lodged there. Ask the dentist or hygienist to show you how to use it properly.

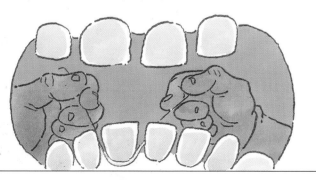

3 MOUTHWASHING

A swish and swash with mouthwash helps to remove plaque, kill germs, and improve oral hygiene. It also reduces the likelihood of bad breath. This is usually caused by bits of food stuck in the mouth, going bad and rotten – like an oral compost heap!

YOU SMELL – IT'S NATURAL Each human body has its own distinctive odor. But exactly how much it smells is up to its owner. Too much of the wrong smell can make a person unpopular, because others avoid their nasty odor. This is where washing and hygiene triumph. Wash your body properly, regularly, and in all the right places, and you can avoid the dreaded B.O. Otherwise your best friend might not stick around for too long.

PROFESSOR'S FACT
WHAT IS B.O.?

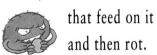

- Body odor is a mixture of smells:
- Old sweat still on skin – not so much the sweat itself, but the bacteria that feed on it and then rot.
- Natural scents of sebum and skin oils, as they collect and become stale.
- Dirt, dust, grime, smears, and substances picked up by the skin.
- All of the above rubbed into clothes that aren't washed. Sometimes it's not B.O. at all, it's C.O. – clothes odor.

INSENSIBLE SWEAT

Skin sweat glands make perspiration or sweat, to cool the body. The hotter you get, the more you sweat. But there's also "background sweating" that happens all the time, even in cold conditions. It's called insensible perspiration and it produces 1 pint (half a liter) daily. So even when you're cool, you're sweaty!

WHERE SWEATS MOST?

Sweat glands are more common in some parts of the skin, compared to others. So these areas sweat most, like the forehead, temples, armpits, palms, groin, backs of the knees, and soles of the feet.

Sweat cannot dry or evaporate from some parts, like the armpits, groin, and feet, since these are usually covered. Instead, it builds up in these areas – so they're the ones you should wash really well.

BIG TIP
NO COVER-UP

Perfumes, scents, and deodorants can help to cover up natural body smells, for a while. But they soon wear off, and they aren't the sole answer. There's no substitute for a good wash with water and soap. Put on the scent afterward, if you want.

THE WALKING ZOO You are covered in thousands of tiny animals, including fleas, lice, mites, ticks, worms, and other mini-beasts who are just trying to survive. They look for a meal of blood and fluids – and you might be the main course. These mini-monsters can get picked up from pets or farm animals, or a walk in the country or town. Most times, you know about them from an itchy bite or spot, where they bite to suck. Get rid of them quickly and easily, with a suitable soap or shampoo.

FLEAS

Most flea bites come from pet fleas. Not fleas that are pets, but fleas from pets, like cats and dogs. These long-jumping insects stray to human skin and suck a meal occasionally, but they usually soon move on. To solve the problem at the source, treat your pets and their bedding with anti-flea powders or sprays.

MICE LICE

Mice are tiny and pale. They live in hair and suck blood … No, hang on, mice are small furry rodents. LICE are tiny and pale, live in hair, and suck blood. These insects lay eggs called nits, which are glued strongly to hairs. An anti-louse shampoo should get rid of them.

MICE MITES

These are arachnids, micro-cousins of spiders. There are hundreds of kinds. The scabies mite burrows into skin, lays its eggs, and causes REALLY ANNOYING ITCHING. These can be treated with a special soap to kill the poor little mites.

BIG TIP
FAMILY MATTERS

Sometimes people seem to catch skin pests again and again. It may be that other family members or close friends also have them, and the pests just get passed around. Ask the doctor or pharmacist, who'll advise the proper treatment. Then make sure other people in close contact get treated, too.

WHY ARE TOESES LIKE NOSES? They both smell! Feet are usually stuck in socks and shoes, away from fresh air. If you don't wash them regularly, and change socks often, they get sweaty, smelly, spotty, and sore. A spot on the sole can be a pain, as the weight of the whole body squashes down on it. So wash feet daily with plenty of soap and warm water. Use fingers or a brush to get dirt and lint from around the toes. (If you're ticklish, this can make you laugh, too!)

ATHLETE'S FOOT

This doesn't just affect athletes – anyone can get it. A type of mold or fungus, *tinea*, grows in the moist skin, especially between the toes. It's irritating and itchy. Wash your feet extra carefully, and use a special powder from the pharmacist.

SPOT NO.7 - THE VERRUCA

This is like a wart in the thick skin of the sole. It feels like a sharp pebble in your shoe! Ask the pharmacist for a cream or ointment to get rid of it.

SPOT NO.8 - THE CORN

This is a foot's self-defense. When something rubs on the foot for a long time, it defends itself by growing very thick skin. Corn pads relieve pressure, and ointments can help too.

SPOT NO.9 - THE BLISTER

Blisters can form anywhere on the skin, after sudden unexpected pressure and rubbing. But don't burst a blister – protect instead it with a soft dressing or a Band-Aid.

PROFESSOR'S FACT
FLAT FEET - WHO CARES?

Some people have "flat feet," where the curve or arch on the inner, lower foot is slightly flatter than normal. However, flat feet still provide people with enough "bounce" to move, walk, and run as normal.

HINTS AND TIPS
CHOOSE SHOES

There are thousands of different styles of shoes, from rugged boots to tottering high heels. Whichever you pick, make sure you select the right shoes for the right job and that they fit properly. If not, they could cause all sorts of trouble.

a healthy DIET

You eat what you are... No, you are what you eat. So healthy food makes a healthy you. Variety is the key. A wide range of foods, especially fresh fruit and veg, is a vital part of a healthy life.

CARS NEED GASOLINE AND SPARES Gasoline contains energy, in chemical form, to make cars go. And the spares replace worn-out parts, like the tires and exhaust. You don't need gasoline or spares. But you do need food, and it does the same two jobs. First, food provides the energy to keep the human body alive, moving, and active. Second, food provides many kinds of nutrients and raw materials, so the body can grow, maintain itself, and replace old or worn parts.

DIGESTION

This is the process of eating food, chewing and swallowing it, mixing it with acids and juices in the stomach and intestines, breaking it down into pieces, and absorbing these into the blood where they are spread around the body. The journey begins at the mouth and ends at the anus.

PROFESSOR'S FACT
HOW LONG IS DIGESTION?

• About 30 feet (9 m) and 24 hours. The whole digestive system, from mouth to anus, is one long tube that is tightly packed into your abdomen, the part of your body sitting just below the rib cage. Food takes an entire day to get through this tube, from eating at one end and excreting at the other. Some foods, especially fatty ones, take a little longer to digest.

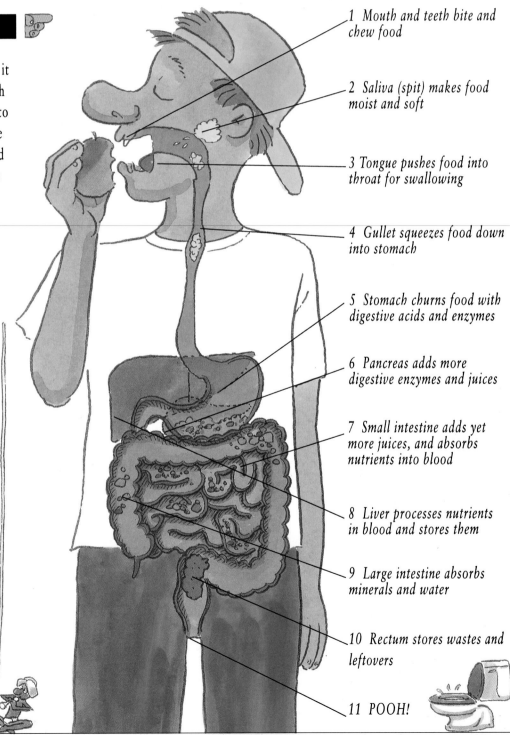

1 Mouth and teeth bite and chew food

2 Saliva (spit) makes food moist and soft

3 Tongue pushes food into throat for swallowing

4 Gullet squeezes food down into stomach

5 Stomach churns food with digestive acids and enzymes

6 Pancreas adds more digestive enzymes and juices

7 Small intestine adds yet more juices, and absorbs nutrients into blood

8 Liver processes nutrients in blood and stores them

9 Large intestine absorbs minerals and water

10 Rectum stores wastes and leftovers

11 POOH!

MUNCH, GULP, SLURP Grab a quick bite here, sip a fast slurp there. No time to waste on eating and drinking, eh? Your body wouldn't agree. It looks forward to a good meal. It's designed to take it easy while you are eating and drinking, and just after. Your body needs time to chew the food properly in its mouth, swallow it without rushing and choking, and digest and absorb the nutrients thoroughly in its stomach and intestines. So make a meal of mealtimes, take them slowly – and enjoy!

THE BIG BREAKFAST

The body does not like to wait for many hours after waking for its first proper meal. A good and varied breakfast brings fresh supplies of energy and nutrients, and gets the digestion going well. And at the end of the day, a huge late meal can overload the digestive system and disrupt sleep.

SPECIAL DIETS

Some athletes eat special types of meals as part of their training, especially food that is high in energy to keep them going. But don't try this at home. At least, not without proper advice from a qualified coach or dietician. It could do more harm than good.

HINTS AND TIPS
RUMMY TUMBLES

When you're hungry, your insides sometimes make strange rumblings and bubblings. As the empty stomach and intestines prepare to digest, they squirm and churn, and slurp and slop the juices and gas within. These gurgling noises are called borborygmus.

LIFE'S A GAS

Buuuurp. Pardon! As you eat a meal, you may swallow up to 1 pint (half a liter) of air. This can come up from the stomach as a belch. Also, the digestive processes make gases such as methane, called flatus. These pockets of air go through the intestines and are pushed out when you pass wind.

BIG TIP
BLOOD'N'MEALS

When you eat a meal, lots of extra blood flows to your stomach and intestines. This carries away the digested nutrients. Less blood is then available for other body parts, like muscles. This is why people who are too active after a meal may get a cramp.

HAS YOUR GET-UP-AND-GO GOT UP AND GONE? If so, maybe you don't eat enough energy foods. They contain the nutrients known as carbohydrates (because they are made mainly of carbon, hydrogen, and oxygen). The main carbohydrate-rich foods are starches and sugars. They are digested and broken down in the body to form the simplest type of sugar – glucose, also called blood sugar. This is the main form of energy used by all the body parts.

PROFESSOR'S FACT
HOW MUCH DO YOU USE?

• Energy is measured in calories. The more active you are, the more energy you burn. On average:

• One minute of lying still, doing nothing, uses about 6 calories.

• One minute of walking uses about 7 calories.

• One minute of fast running uses 15 calories.

SWEET SUGAR

Any food that tastes sweet usually has lots of sugar. This is almost instant energy. The sugars in chocolate, sweets, candies, jams, cakes, and cookies are absorbed quickly by the body. But these foods have little else in the way of nutrients. And they're usually bad for your teeth! Some vegetables and fruits are also sugary. They contain many other nutrients that are good for the body, so they make a much better alternative for you.

SUPER-STARCHES

Starchy foods include cereals and grains such as wheat and rice, bread, pasta, potatoes, and some fruit and vegetables. They take longer to digest than pure sugars, so they provide more sustained energy. And if they're made using wholemeal or wholegrain, they will also supply useful vitamins, minerals, and fiber.

HINTS AND TIPS
ENERGY SNAX

How much energy will a snack give you? In calories:

• Apple 81

• Banana 105

• Chocolate bar 1,000

• Chips (bag) 600

• Crunchy cereal bar 200

• Ice cream scoop 400

• Peanuts (packet) 1,000

• Yogurt 250

THE PROFESSOR SAYS: "EAT PROTEIN!" Not because that's his name, but because a wide variety of protein-rich food is healthy for you. Proteins are the body's main structural substances. They form its framework of bones, and make up its muscles, nerves, and other working parts. Proteins are also needed for growth, maintenance, and repair of these body tissues. They add taste, flavor, and "satisfaction" to meals. There are two main kinds – from plants and animals.

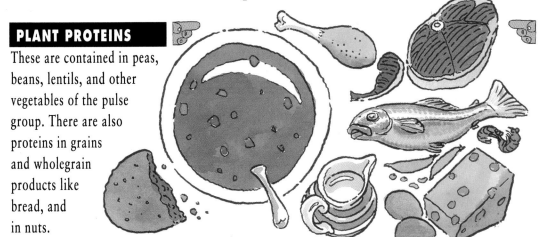

PLANT PROTEINS

These are contained in peas, beans, lentils, and other vegetables of the pulse group. There are also proteins in grains and wholegrain products like bread, and in nuts.

ANIMAL PROTEINS

Animal proteins are found in all kinds of meat. These include red meat such as beef and lamb, and white meat including pork, chicken, and other poultry. They are also found in fish, shellfish, seafood, and dairy products such as milk and eggs.

PROFESSOR'S FACT
BREAK DOWN, BUILD UP

Proteins are made of subunits or building blocks called amino acids. These are similar in both plant and animal proteins. You break down and digest the proteins in your food, into the separate amino acids. Your body then sticks these amino acids back together in a different order, to make your own body parts.

BIG TIP
FOOD ALLERGIES

Some people are extrasensitive or allergic to certain foods. They may break out in a skin rash or have digestive pains. But it may be difficult to identify the exact substance causing the problem, since so many prepared foods have lots of ingredients and additives. Get advice from a dietary expert and try eating a selection of fresh, natural, unprocessed, unpackaged foods.

MAKE NO MISTAKE – YOU NEED TO EAT FAT But not too much. Fats, oils, and similar substances, known as lipids, are vital for the body. The billions of microscopic body cells have thin "skins," or membranes, that are partly made from lipids. They are also important for nerves and other body parts. But don't forget, also, that too much fat is bad for you, especially animal fats.

ANIMAL FATS

There are two main kinds of animal fats. Those in red meats and dairy products, like butter and cheese, are called saturated fats. Those in poultry and fish are called unsaturated fats. Unsaturated fats are slightly healthier than saturated fats. But too much of either can cause problems for the heart, blood vessels, and blood.

HINTS AND TIPS
CUT DOWN ON FAT

• Eat less burgers, salamis, patés, and other fatty meats.

• Eat less butter, cream, high-fat cheeses, and other dairy foods that are high in fat.

PROFESSOR'S FACT
WHAT'S BODY FAT?

• You body has a layer of fat called adipose tissue. It is thicker in some parts, such as the buttocks. Just under the skin, this layer helps to keep in body warmth. It also forms soft cushions against damaging injuries. However, if you eat too much food (of any kind), the extra is converted into fat and stored as flabby lumps. This makes you obese or "fat."

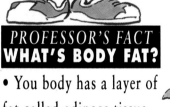

POLYUNSATURATED FATS

PLANT FATS

Various plants and their products contain fats or oils, such as olives, sunflowers, corn, and avocado. These oils are called polyunsaturated fats. They are healthier than both saturated or unsaturated fats. But again, too much of any kind of fat can cause health problems.

LESS FAT, MORE THIN

The body usually uses carbohydrates to get most of its energy. But if these are in short supply in its food, it turns to fats, since they contain lots of energy too. Any fat stored in the adipose tissue is broken down and used up for energy. This is why a diet makes you thinner.

• Eat less foods prepared with fat or oil. Avoid chips, fried foods, cakes, and cookies.

ALMOST ANY FOOD IS HEALTHY, provided you eat the right amount of it. You can eat certain types of food as much as you want. They include fresh fruit, vegetables, and nuts. They are healthy because they contain plenty of vitamins and minerals. These are special nutrients that the body needs to stay well and fight off disease. Eating lots of different types of food, with the correct amounts of nutrients is called a balanced diet. Fruit and vegetables should form a large part of this.

MINERALS

Like vitamins, minerals are only needed in small amounts. They include calcium which is good for teeth and bones, iron for blood, and iodine for hormones. Once again, anyone who eats a wide range of foods should get enough. If you're young and growing, dairy products are a good source, too.

VITAMINS

The body needs about 20 main vitamins, but only in small amounts. Many of them are vital for the complex chemical life processes that occur inside body cells. Without them, the body will suffer from vitamin deficiency diseases such as rickets and scurvy.

YOU CAN'T EAT SUNSHINE

True. But some sunshine can add to your diet. Exposure to sunlight helps the body to manufacture a vitamin for itself. This is vitamin D. It is made by the skin, and needed for healthy bones. But of course – not too much sunshine, or you'll risk other health problems (☞ Nº22).

BIG TIP
VIT&MIN TABS

Some people take tablets or supplements of concentrated vitamins and minerals. This is unlikely to cause harm, providing you follow the package instructions. With an ordinary diet, many times the required amounts of vitamins are provided.

PROFESSOR'S FACT
VITAMIN C

• Ascorbic acid, or vitamin C, is found in fresh vegetables and fruits, especially blackcurrants and citrus fruits such as oranges. Scientists are not sure if it helps the body fight infection. But they do know that it's needed for healthy skin and gums. Another good reason for fresh fruit as a snack!

FIBER IS USELESS, AND USEFUL The fiber, bulk or roughage in food is mainly formed from tough plant materials, such as cellulose. It contains little nutritional value. It can't be digested and broken down to give you proteins or carbohydrates. In fact, it makes up most of the leftovers at the end of digestion. But fiber is still very important. It makes the digestion work more efficiently and regularly, and it may protect against certain illnesses. So eat it and excrete it!

PROFESSOR'S FACT
THE RUNS

• Diarrhea is passing runny, watery feces. It may be due to:

• gut infection

• certain foods, such as prunes or beans

• bad, disagreeable foods

• stress, excitement, or nervousness

• certain medical drugs.

Most attacks pass in a day. If not, or if there's great gut pain, or blood in the feces, see the doc.

HOW FIBER HELPS

Fiber gives bulk and substance to the food as it's being digested. This allows the intestines to massage and move it, helping to exercise the intestine muscles at the same time. Fiber slows food's passage, giving time for digestion. It helps to carry away wastes, as feces (stools or bowel movements) which are soft and easily squished out. It may also protect against diseases such as colon cancer.

HIGH-FIBER FOODS

As usual, fresh vegetables have plenty of fiber, especially pulses, like beans and lentils, leafy vegetables, and some fruits, and wholemeal and wholegrain (unrefined) cereals and their products, like bran, wholemeal breads, and wholegrain granola bars also do.

TOO MUCH FIBER?

Yes, some people have eaten too much fiber – but it's very difficult! Vast amounts of fiber, at the expense of other nutrients, can cause problems absorbing certain minerals from food.

HINTS AND TIPS
BEING "REGULAR"

Some people empty their bowels (defecate) every two or three days. Others do so two or three times a day. No problem, provided it's regular and painless. Plenty of fiber helps to bulk out the feces and stop the feces from becoming too hard and painful to pass, called constipation.

IS JUNK FOOD REALLY JUNK? Probably not. Foods like burgers, hot dogs, and potato chips provide their own selection of nutrients. Eaten now and again, as part of a balanced diet, they are fine. But the same narrow choice of food, day after day, causes problems. Whether it's burgers, or potato chips, or carrots, or celery – the same stuff all the time is bad news for the body. Variety is the spice of life and the key to healthy eating.

PROFESSOR'S FACT
NEED A DRINK?

• The body needs about 4 pints (2 liters) of water every day, to stay alive. Since the food you eat is about two-thirds water, you don't need to drink all this! Be careful to drink more if you're exercising or active, or if it's too hot and sweaty, as your body will need more water. Lack of fluids, called dehydration, can be very

10 BIG TIPS FOR
HEALTHY EATING

1 Eat a wide variety of foods. You might like some of them!

2 Put time aside for meals, rather than eating on the run.

3 Chew each mouthful well. It helps taste, digestion, and excretion!

4 Eat plenty of fresh vegetables and fruits.

5 Don't eat too many fatty foods.

6 Have some breakfast, rather than "running on empty" for many hours.

7 Don't cook foods to death. Prolonged boiling, especially, washes out nutrients, vitamins, and minerals.

8 For the odd snack, don't always reach for chocolate or chips. Try some fruit or a granola bar.

9 Don't forget the fiber.

10 Watch your weight. Use a height-weight chart to see if you are overweight. If so, eat less fats and sugars, and exercise more.

EAT MORE FOOD

THE DANGERS OF DIRT Germs love dirt. They get on dirty hands – or dirty anything – and might get onto your food and into your mouth. Once inside your guts, the germs love the warm, wet, nourishing conditions. They multiply like crazy and cause food poisoning, with stomachache, vomiting, and diarrhea. Ouch, yuk, puke! We'd rather have the food without the poisoning.

BETTER OUT THAN IN

Funny tummy. Feel a bit sick. Cold face. Churning belly. Brp, ugg, retch, uurrghh! Splat. The technical name for throwing up, or vomiting, is reverse peristalsis, squeezing stomach contents up the gullet and out through the mouth. It's the body's natural way of getting rid of bad food, too much food, germs on food, and any other unwanted stuff.

PROFESSOR'S FACT
SAFELY COVERED

• Cooks and chefs who handle food must be incredibly careful about hygiene. Customers would be very upset if they started to get food poisoning. Professional chefs cover cuts and sores with blue Band-aids. If these fall off accidentally, they can be seen easily as not many foods are blue! Cuts on hands mean having to wear special gloves, or not handling food at all.

CLEAN TOOLS AND TOWELS

Even if food itself is clean and well prepared, a dirty fork or plate can spread germs. So wash cutlery, crockery, and utensils in hot soapy water (or in the dishwasher). Dish-towels must be clean, as well.

WHY WASH HANDS?

Germs float in the air and settle on almost everything, including you. Washing with soap and water won't make things perfectly germ-free forever. But it sure cuts down the risks. If you're preparing food, scrub fingernails too. There could be a million germs under each one!

HINTS AND TIPS
TRUST YOUR INSTINCTS

If a food looks suspicious, smells bad, or tastes foul, don't risk it. Avoid it. (This applies especially to brussel sprouts.) The human senses of sight, smell, and taste evolved over millions of years, partly to warn us that some things were bad to eat. Trust your gut feeling!

WOULD YOU PADDLE IN EXCREMENT And then stomp on your food before you eat it? Flies do, given the chance. And they have six legs, four more than you. So keep flies and other pests away from your meals. Especially, keep meats cool in sealed containers, so flies can't lay their eggs on them. Otherwise the eggs hatch into maggots and you'll have to fight them for the meal. Stop them by storing and cooking food properly.

NO BLOWING OR DRIBBLING

You wouldn't blow your nose on food or dribble on it. So, when you're preparing or making food, try not to sneeze or cough over it. This would blast thousands of tiny mucus droplets at the food. Other people don't want to eat your mucus or spit.

KEEP IT COOL

Most foods are kept cool in a refrigerator. This slows down the bacteria that make your food spoil. However, it does not stop them, and the food will turn bad eventually. If you want to keep food for a long time then it needs to be frozen in a freezer.

BIG TIPS
GOOD COOKING

• If food can be stored, keep it cool and covered or contained. The refrigerator is ideal for this job.

• Cook food thoroughly. You never know whether some food contains eggs, germs, or worms.

• Reheat food quickly, and thoroughly at a high temperature.

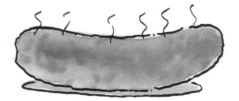

• Never re-freeze food that's already been frozen and then thawed.

EVERY DAY, IN EVERY WAY, the human body needs looking after. After all, car owners spend lots of time checking their vehicles, changing the oil, maintaining and fixing the engine, and cleaning and polishing the body. But do they show the same care for their own bodies? To keep the human body clean and healthy, and on the road to a long and happy life, it needs regular attention and maintenance.

DOWN-TIME

Do not strain the brain or control systems by too many hours of continuous usage. Allow regular periods of rest and sleep.

FUEL INTAKE

Clean teeth twice or more daily. Insert into mouth reasonable quantities of healthy, balanced foods and drinks. Not too much fat, not too little fiber. Regular mealtimes recommended, but not overeating – overweight strains body systems.

BODYWORK

Wash regularly with soap and water, in the shower or bath. Clean dirt out of cracks and crevices. Avoid build-up of coolants like sweat. Brush or comb hair to get rid of tangles and dirt.

RECEPTOR SYSTEMS

Have a dental checkup every 6-12 months, and an eye exam every year or so, too. Be aware of dulled hearing. Report suspicions or malfunctions to your doctor.

POWER UNITS AND INTERNAL SYSTEMS

Maintain muscles in active working order by regular exercise. This also keeps the heart pump, blood pipes, and lung bellows functioning efficiently.

CHASSIS AND COUPLINGS

Regular activity and exercise will keep bones strong and joints supple.

Aerobic respiration – A form of producing energy that needs oxygen to work.

Anaerobic respiration – A form of producing energy that does not need oxygen to work.

Blood – The fluid that flows to all parts of your body, carrying nutrients. It is made up of tiny blood cells and a watery fluid, called plasma.

Bone – A solid part of the body that supports and protects the flabby parts. Together, the different bones in your body form your skeleton.

Breathing – The action that inflates your lungs and draws in air.

Carbohydrate – A substance made from carbon, hydrogen, and oxygen. Carbohydrates include sugars.

Cool down – A routine you should do when you have finished exercising. It relaxes the joints and muscles, and stops them from becoming stiff.

Digestion – The process of chewing, swallowing, breaking down, absorbing, and excreting food. The whole process takes place in your digestive system.

Exercise – Any activity that works your muscles, including your heart and lungs. It can increase your stamina, strength, and suppleness.

Fiber – The undigestable part of your food. It allows your intestines to massage the food through them.

Joint – Any point where two bones meet. These can be inflexible, such as the joints between your skull bones, or very flexible, like your hip.

Ligament – A tough fiber that holds the bones close together at joints, preventing them from moving too far apart, or dislocating.

Lung – One of two organs in your chest that air is breathed into and oxygen can be absorbed.

Muscle – A part of your body that is able to get smaller or contract. Muscles pull on the bones in your limbs to move you about.

Protein – A complicated substance that can be broken down by your body into smaller parts, called amino acids, and then rebuilt to form body parts.

Pulse – Also called your heartbeat, this is the rhythm that your heart beats at. It's measured in beats per minute.

Skeleton – The internal structure of your body that supports its shape. It is made from over 200 separate bones.

Soap – A special chemical, also called a detergent, which attaches itself to dirt and breaks it into smaller parts. Soap can be used to get you clean.

Stamina – The period of time you can exercise is a measure of your stamina. The greater your stamina, the fitter you are and the longer you can last.

Strength – The capacity of your muscles to lift heavier weights or pull greater loads is a measure of your strength.

Suppleness – A measure of the flexibility of your limbs and joints.

Tendon – A ropelike fiber that attaches your muscles to your bones.

Vitamin – A substance that your body needs in tiny amounts. These help to run the body's processes.

Warm-up – A routine you must do before you exercise. It gets the blood flowing to the muscles and prevents any pulls and strains.